Civilization On Trial

or

The True Path

to a

Christian Democracy

By Mat Klaren

PRICE, 20 Cents

Published by
The Christian Democracy Publishing Company
Fort Wayne, Indiana.

504741

Dedication

To the men and women the world over, who, like the pioneers of yesterday, see the beautiful valleys beyond the mountains of today.

To the men and women of all lands, for their delightful dreams and lovely thoughts, showing a light beyond, a vision, creating the star of hope, as a guide for us all.

To the babes born and unborn, to the youths of all oncoming ages, who will inherit the earth and all its fruits, who will enter, on account of our efforts, into a promised land, a new garden of Eden, a paradise lost.

To all of these, this little book is dedicated.

THE AUTHOR.

Preface

Down through the ages, God has always sent his messenger to every race, into every clime, to prepare them for that which is to come. He sent a Moses to liberate Israel, a Christ to liberate the world, a Washington to liberate a freedom-loving people and a Lincoln to liberate the black slave.

Did ever a bee or butterfly realize the reaper's coming or the winter's dawn, the destroyer of the sweetness of their lives, as they fly from flower to flower?

Did ever man, the prince of creation, endowed with power and glory, realize the minute of his exit from the scenes of strife?

Did ever woman, the mother of men, casting to the winds in utter abandon the most sacred gift of nature, realize what her children will say on the day they grasp the harm produced?

Did ever king, or czar, in purple splendor, the emblem of ancient regal power, realize the time of his helpless resignation?

Did ever a civilization, governed, strong and fearless, realize the hour of its undoing?

Did ever we, in a thoughtful mood, think of the danger that confronts us now, think of what tomorrow might bring, or will we, like civilizations past, let ourselves drift over the brink of a bottomless gulf?

The time is now, that we must realize the danger that faces our civilization, our nation and our individualism, that we must build the future upon a foundation of truth and justice or surrender to the past and to oblivion.

Introduction

Man, the superb handiwork of all creation, because of intellect, in his zeal to become the master of land, sea and air, converted vast prairies into fields of golden grain; transformed mighty forests into fruits and flowers; burrowed tunnels through the mountains for broad, smooth highways; drilled into the bowels of the earth to enslave her hidden treasures; builded complete cities into single crafts to ride the stormy seas; pierced the dizzy heights with heavier than air machines; harnessed the hidden and mysterious energies of electricity; united the forces of nature with creatures of steel and gave to his creations power, force and life to operate at his direction.

He looked upon his handiwork with pride, and said: "It is well". He believed he had wrestled from nature her secrets and had enslaved her power—for man and man's comfort and pleasure. He saw reflected in the mirrors of his creation what he interpreted to be the power of man.

In the pride of his greatness he could not see his failure. While he had enslaved nature, he had also enslaved himself to the Monsters of his own creation. He had become the victim of his own prowess; a prey for thieves and vultures who direct the energies of his own handiwork.

Man of intellect, yet so busy with his creative genius that he could not see the struggle for existence was growing more acute with the passing of each day's sun; that it was fast becoming impossible with the rapidly growing complexity of the industrial system which he had built to successfully engage in the battle of life, of food, clothing and shelter, as an individual; that the power of his creation was withering the flower of his individual opportunity.

Man of intellect today—bewildered, confused, living in fear of the morrow. Powerful man on the verge of destruction by his own creations.

No longer can man live alone. His life must blend into the lives of others, and others into his. Others he must serve and others must serve him. The strong must protect the weak and the weak must cooperate with the strong. They must not be enslaved by them. One for all and all for one. The question, "Am I my Brother's Keeper"? The Answer, "There is neither Jew nor Greek, there is neither bond nor free, there is neither male nor female, for we are all one."

In every age social and economic changes have occurred which have given the student and thinker cause for grave concern. He has looked at the picture of what has been, what is now and dreamed of what should be and has speculated as to how near society might provide the answer to the dream.

In the high spirit of individualism man seldom pauses long enough to appraise his importance as a cog in the great machine of social justice or to fully appreciate his responsibility as a member of society, a citizen of the State and a unit of a Common Brotherhood.

In this mighty nation of over 120,000,000 people, men have been trying to govern themselves in such manner as to enjoy the fullness of life in the light of peace, happiness and contentment. In this effort they have *not* succeeded. When we fail, there must be a cause for failure. Every result or effect has a cause, and if the effect is bad, there must be a remedy for the cause producing it.

Governments are the products of the human race and have been builded step by step. They have been grounded upon human intelligence, and out of that intelligence has grown organizations which we choose to call Governments.

Governments as the result of human association, are effective only as human intelligence has been constructively applied to economic developments in the social structure from generation to generation. Men create Governments. Governments regulate society and society charts the course of human relations and associations, either toward the star of hope or the clouds of despair.

In its inception those who conceived this nation created a society and social structure representative of truth, honor and justice, based upon the Declaration of Independence and expressed in the Constitution of the United States.

In the last few years the star of hope has dimmed, the clouds of despair have thickened. Human intelligence has ceased to function unselfishly and therefore it is well for us to examine ourselves, our Government, our society, and to analyze, as best we can, the tendency of the human race in its course of development, in order that a permanent cure for a very sick human race may be found.

Table of Contents

***

CHAPTER I.

The Human Race

In the morning of human activity, when the race was yet in its infancy, the cry of human want was only food, shelter, rest and sleep. Wants were simple and there were no complicated desires nor any exorbitant expectations. Everything was of the simplest form. The germ of mind had not yet formed initiative. It too was in its infancy. To a child in its crib, it matters little what promise the future may hold in store, on account of heritage, family, social position, or financial expectancy. It must pass through the stages of infancy, just as the most lowly of babes. Likewise the human race had to pass through the stages of its infancy. In all the days of its childhood, little by little and step by step, did the human race constructively and progressively wend its way to the heights which it has now attained. Time and space counted for naught. Nothing counted except force. First physical force, later mental force, but always, force. In this development mistakes were made and many of them, but they were constructive in character, in that they furnished a guide for further development. Had they been destructive, the race would have

13

destroyed itself. Only when obstructions hindered progress, did destruction take place. When constructive action was paramount, the race was happy and satisfied, and when destruction appeared, the race was disturbed and unhappy.

At first mental development and intellectual advance was slow, until it arrived at a certain place where it seemed to have accumulated enough information to develop by leaps and bounds. During these periods the human intellect developed more in the course of a year than it seemed to have developed in the course of a century before.

As in the building of a mighty structure, every stone discovered misplaced means more to the perfect completion than all of the science in its creation.

As the mind developed, the human race acquired new methods. It began to seek ways and means of lightening the burdens of toil that had accumulated as the result of physical application. Active intellect and intelligence began the search for a new course in the securing of human wants, human desires, and their relation to human happiness.

With the simplicity of wants, the race lived in a rather ignorant happiness, perhaps similar to a paradise such as is enjoyed by the birds, the bees and the bear. Nature provided for wants (food, rest and sleep) but not without risk. When the food harvest had passed, food became exhausted and deprivation and want became the dominant fear. When rest and sleep were disturbed by real or imaginary dangers, discontent arose which caused the mind to become active, in the development of security in every activity provided by nature. In this development many methods were tried and divers applications of methods resorted to. Thought after thought was analyzed, rejected or adopted and dream after dream tested, until it had run its course, discarded only to be picked up in another form, and tried again and again. Slowly but surely progress became apparent. Race after race perished, civilization after civilization disappeared, but each time elevating a succeeding race or a succeeding civilization to a higher plane. In this development there were many retarding, visible and invisible forces, but throughout the centuries more constructive than destructive effort has been the result, as taking two steps forward and one backward. In the end the human race has succeeded in going onward, forward and upward, slowly, but surely. At first crude tools of wood, rock or flint, coarsely constructed, were used in an effort to supply human wants. Later came more scientific and accurate mechanical construction, but always those tools were owned by him who made them and used them.

A new day has developed a new method. Tools are complicated, made for mass production, owned by a few, operated by a few, creating tremendous wealth in concentrated form and resulting in the exploitation of the entire human race.

Concentration of wealth and exploitation of humankind is the disease which is eating out the vitals of society, threatening destruction unless a cure can be found. Common ownership of the tools of production and the fair distribution of the wealth created by the efforts of the producer, scientifically managed, with an equitable distribution of earnings and wealth, is the first step in effecting the cure of the disease.

Exploitation has no place in society, wrongs in economic development cannot be justified. The race desires to be happy and has a right to live in a world safe, sane, satisfying, full of love and peace. Human intelligence, properly applied, can create such a world. Nature has provided the resources and it is only by misdirection of effort that hunger, want and despair have become the dominant fear of the age. Remove the cause and we move to a higher plane, building always onward and upward, for the benefit of the race, having in mind the welfare of all.

Individualism must of necessity be submerged in group welfare. Under our theory of Government, every citizen is sovereign in his own right. Let us make him a sovereign in fact. A mighty factor in the universal scheme of things; a fit and harmonious subject of existence as a unit in a new and better world, where the bitter fruit of hatred shall have withered and the dastardly aims of selfishness shall have been destroyed; where one great and happy family shall have been created, so that the forces of nature shall be enslaved to serve, in order that man may have his most cherished desires without injury to the least or most lowly.

Such is the aim of the human race, the desire of civilization. The problem is a human problem, to be solved by men. It may be done now or we may defer action into the distant future. Time and space count for naught, force and intelligence is all that matters. Civilization trembles on the brink of despair. Let it not destroy itself.

CHAPTER II.

Man

The most beautiful romance in the world is woven into the story of man, as he laughs or as he weeps, as he climbs to the highest pinnacle of fame, as he goes down to the lowest depths of depravity, as he soars into the clouds on his hopes, or slumps into the valley of despair, as he glories over his success, or broods over his failure, as the tides of his loves and his hates ebb and flow as he ever follows the star of his hope toward the goal of his loftiest ideals and into the realms of the most fanciful of dreams.

Somewhere, by some power in the universe, life is created, we know not why, where, or when, but this we do know, that in the ever changing civilization, the onward march of man, the prince of creation, was prone to do everything wrong until he injured himself. Out of the errors he would outline a new path toward progress, following a sort of natural law of going the route of least resistance.

Nature is not perfect, if it were, perhaps it would not rain in the ocean. This law of following the paths of least resistance does not apply to intellectual development of civilization, but rather to life without culture and of inferior intellect.

Man's first food consisted of roots, herbs, fruits and nuts produced by nature. He did not eat meat until his natural food became scarce. Instead of cultivating the soil and producing the natural food now enjoyed by man, he ate fish easily caught, invented the bow and arrow and ate game easily killed, following the path of least resistance, changing from a vegetarian to a carnivorous creature, even in some instances becoming a cannibal and eating his own kind. When man comes to the fullest realization of his intellectual and mental powers, he will not have to rely upon physical force, and he will become what his Creator intended him to become. Intellectual man will free himself from the shackles that bind him to a system destroying happiness and will become a sovereign, a master, a superior to all creation, as nature intended.

CHAPTER III.

Woman

Woman, the burden carrier of man, ever held in slavery by him and ever crushed in her attempt to attain self freedom, now, as throughout the ages, ministers to his wants, without stint, selfishness or malice. Everything has she done for him and little has he done in return. Her soft, skilled hands comfort, heal, soothe and please. The touch of her fingers change the hard sick bed to down and dreams, and her soft caress changes the tears of childhood to happy smiles. It is woman who brings man as a babe through the paths strewn with roses, and when life's work is done, sweetens the gateway for the soul to enter the unknown world.

Man has always taunted her as an inferior and ruled her as a slave. If she failed, he became a savage and a barbarian. It was woman who was the creator of the modern world, the inventor of agriculture, music and art. Without her, life would lose its charm. It is she who bears the future in her body and nurses life to its highest form.

The future should hold a happy vision and the star of hope should be bright for her. In the last decade she has freed herself from many shackles. If she comprehended her power today, she would rule the world. She now stands on a parity with man. No longer shall she be regarded as private property, but a free person as man himself and ever acting as his guide to the future destiny of the race, and to those loftier, nobler and higher ideals which bring peace, contentment and happiness into the lives and hearts of men. She deserves, and in the future shall have opportunity to share in the common blessings of the race, where love, beauty, peace and plenty shall replace hate, despair, want, poverty and war.

Man shall build the house and woman shall make it home, for all time to come.

CHAPTER IV.

Civilization.

In the dawn of civilization man roamed the forests and the plains in search of food and fray, alone. Ignorant and superstitious he wandered from place to place, misunderstanding and distrusting everything with which he came in contact. He desired companionship, and the first step toward progressive civilization was taken when he organized the gen and began to live a cooperative life. One for all and all for one led by the strongest man of the gen, the one who could wield the largest club. Then came the tribe where he again lived a cooperative life, but where the wise man ruled, the old men of the tribe. When a child was born, it was born to the tribe, and adopted by it. When food became scarce the tribe moved to new locations and hunger caused them to force their way against all opposition. These tribes became larger and grew more powerful, and eventually governments were formed. Thus were born kingdoms. In these kingdoms greed for power made rulers tyrants, and to this tyranny subjects submitted, sought favors and slavery was conceived as a result of special privilege extended to those held in especial esteem. In this development freedom, cooperation and brotherhood were in a large measure destroyed and selfishness, hatred, vanity, jealousy, envy and suspicion began to rise and the mental afflictions that are characteristic of the human race began to leave their imprint upon the character builders of the family of men.

Because of intellect the human race responds readily to refined or crude influences, quickly adapts itself to new surroundings and environments, and yields rather promptly to development and progress, or to the blight. In the heart of man there has throughout the ages gradually developed a certain bitterness which the races retained from the harsh barbarious life of the past, bringing to humankind nothing but sorrow, grief and pain. These could be eliminated if selfishness and greed could be removed. "A flower can be coaxed out of any weed", but weeds are weeds so long as they are crushed and trampled upon. If cultivated and cared for they become flowers and bear fruit. The same rule applies to man. Government being the cultivating influence of mankind on account of its regulation of social relationships in order to coax the flowers out of the weeds must be kind, honest, equitable and just, in order that proper environment may be provided and human relationships pleasant. It is a responsibility of government to sufficiently supervise its social and economic institutions to provide that everyone has opportunity to earn good, wholesome food, decent and comfortable clothing, and enjoy sunshine, music and agreeable companionship under such educational facilities as will fit them for a harmonious existence in a land of peace and plenty. When this shall be provided, then the family of man will develop into rational creatures living as God intended that it should live. Were it not so, man's Creator would not have distinguished him from the rest of the animal world by creating, as part of his being, intellect.

CHAPTER V.

Environment and Heredity

As we study the characteristics of man and note the development of his reasoning faculties we begin to search for the reason of his peculiar traits of conduct.

We find that the development of any race is retarded or pushed forward by environment and heredity. Both exert their influence upon the other and they are closely related, each modifying and changing the other.

Environment influences heredity and heredity builds character, traits and peculiarities.

The tribal traits come to us from our remote ancestors, in which we find catalogued fear, superstition and their retarding influences. Also freedom, justice, cooperation and brotherhood with their beneficent influences.

The racial traits giving rise to race prejudice, hatred, selfishness and a desire for self-aggrandizement with the handicaps which follow in their train, and love of race and country which breeds the patriotic influences making possible a unified and compact form of government for the regulation of social conduct.

The family traits which form in a large measure the base of human activity; minds and lives are blended together and out of the blending process comes a new mind and character to be blended with another and again create a new life. It has ever been thus and has been the most interesting process in human development.

When the race was young, man was ruled by superstition and fear. He understood not the course of the sun's daily path through the skies, and became a sun worshipper. Thunder and lightning terrorized him and he looked to the God of Thunder or of Fire to protect him. As he lay on his back and noted the darkness come with the sinking sun, he appealed to the God of Night to protect him. All the phenomena of nature to him was supernatural.

Population was sparce. He had almost complete freedom of the earth. The freedom and fear bred within his nature a desire for companionship and brotherhood. Cooperation was essential to blot out a part of his superstitious fear. Science and education has for centuries been endeavoring to correct the errors of reason on the part of man, premised upon fear.

Racial traits can be obliterated by human brotherhood, and family traits improved by natural selection scientifically directed.

Had early man understood the phenomena of nature he could have saved two thousand years in the building of a world brotherhood where men could live as one happy family. He did not understand. Destiny decreed otherwise. We have a jangled mass of humanity, seething to and fro as the tide, with nothing to do, no place to go, without hope, seeing before them only the fear of the ages dressed in new garb. We have science, education and understanding. We do not use it. It belongs to man. Now it is covered with the wet blanket of selfishness. It *must* be removed and a new race must be built.

Human nature can be, must be and will be modified. Civilization must not perish.

CHAPTER VI.

Economic Changes

Kingdoms were created by man for his own joy, but as time passed they became subservient to the wills and whims of the strong, and grew destructive to the finer mental qualities of man. Along with the building of kingdoms he built vast economic empires.

From Egypt where the Nile overflowed its banks, blotted out the markers for lands and fertilized the valley, came the art of farming, irrigation and surveying.

From the Babylonians, the pioneers of barter and commerce, originated education, reading, writing and arithmetic.

The seafaring Phoenicians gave to us navigation.

The Greeks, with their love for, and practice of liberty, freedom and Democracy, naturally conceived art and music.

From the Romans we inherit the love of conquest, war and domination.

From the Israelites came the love for a living God, truth, justice and spirituality.

From the fact that life originated in the water, we inherit the love for water.

From the savage the love for the forest, the wild and the out-of-doors.

From the barbarian we inherit rudeness, cruelty and ferocity.

From fuedalism, confiscation and exploitation.

From Capitalism we inherit the love for money, riches, and the art of living at the expense of others and the desire to create artificial wealth.

From the Christ we inherit that which is good and true in life and those qualities of character which enable man to live life in its true fullness, if practiced, all grounded upon that basic attribute of character and complete life—love. On love is based all of the beautiful ethics of christianity.

Little wonder it is that with all of the influences of the past which are now blended into the lives and characters of men of the present that the human race is living in a state of bewilderment and chaos. Strange as it may seem, those savage instincts seem at the present time to have predominated and there is not only confusion in the world of ideas but in the world of action. Force, physical force and power now seek to rule the world. Intellect has been submerged in violence. The sword has been substituted for reason. Wars and rumors of wars. Whither bound, civilization?

Man can produce enough for all and to spare in only a fraction of the time required in the yesteryear, yet he suffers from want, malnutrition, distrust and discontent, the products of misdirected intellect, guided by physical power and physical force.

Man, in all his sorrow, is more to be pitied than censured. More sinned against than sinning. Out of the past has come the misery. It has crept upon man with the stealth of an adder in the jungle. Propaganda, controlled by capital, provided the jungle. Man could not get the truth. He does not get it now. Greed for gold by those controlling the dissemination of facts through the press, and even the schools, the adder. Poverty, want and misery—the sting.

The race is ill, very ill. The fever of unrest runs high. A cure must be found if the forward march of civilization is to begin and the rotting processes of retrogression are to be halted.

We must enter into a new era and lay the foundations for a new civilization on human brotherhood and the love of fellowman. We must build a new democracy, a world democracy, wherein war shall be no more, and man and woman will be on equal terms, with justice and science as a guide, develop agriculture, industry, commerce, education and culture for the benefit of and to be enjoyed by all.

Love, music, art must be taught and selfishness, cruelty, exploitation, conquest and domination, which have come to us out of the night of the past, must be destroyed.

Life's noblest ideals must be planted and grown in the fullness of the sun, for love, happiness and contentment.

Warehouses must be filled to meet human requirements, with poverty and want unknown and men must, amid peace and joy, be able to sing in unison as did the angels of Bethlehem at the birth of the greatest emancipator of all times,

"Glory to God in the highest, and on earth peace to men of good will."

CHAPTER VII.

The Dreamer

In those dark ages when woman was a beast of burden for man, he did not dream of tractors with which to plow, combines with which to harvest, locomotives with which to transport his products, automobiles with which to travel, great ships with which to join continents, aeroplanes with which to hurtle him through space, could even become a reality as the product of the efforts of man.

He did realize that his methods were crude, slow, tedious and painful. Dissatisfaction arose in his soul. He began to think and to plan, and as a thinker he began to dream dreams.

A dreamer harnessed the oxen, another the horse. Dreamers harnessed the forces of nature, water, fire, gas and electricity.

It was a dreamer who first in mortal combat saw a meal by becoming a cannibal. Another dreamed of a better way of making slaves of his captives and making them work for him. Another confiscated land as a corollary and fuedalism arose. Then came the superdreamer who acquired the machinery of production and distribution, became an exploiter of the human race and enslaved all but a chosen few.

Now millions of exploited are dreaming dreams of violence, destruction and confusion.

The dreamer enslaved the slave and a dreamer freed him. A dreamer built a system of exploitation and a dreamer will destroy it. The question—in the destruction, will he destroy the race?

A dreamer hollowed a log, made a paddle and floated it on the water; another sawed the log into boards, made a boat to be propelled by galley slaves. A dreamer hoisted a canvas to the wind and freed the galley slave of his toil by harnessing nature's wind, another dreamed the fire and water to produce steam could do it more efficiently and now great ocean palaces daily plow their way through the seas to the farthermost corners of the world, truly making of the world, physically, a family of nations, yet spiritually and intellectually a family of enemies seeking power and gold and more gold— not for the nation, but for a chosen few in each of them.

Sweat, toil, sorrow, blood, war, bitterness, hatred, dreams of lust for gold and power. Millions the tools of the few who control the gold and power. Millions submerged in the greed of a few—otherwise there would be no more war.

Man submissive to the exploitation by greed. He will allow greed and gold to destroy life and happiness when he could prevent it—but will not do so. Strange paradox—man, the dreamer.

Dreamers dreamed and were persecuted and ridiculed therefor. Wright Brothers had to go to France to obtain assistance in perfecting the aeroplane. Their nation would not interpret the dream.

John Hale who dreamed of free public schools and education—ridiculed as a fanatic.

The aristocrat, the exploiter of the time, said: "It is an idle dream. If you educate the common people they will not work".

Education of the common people gave birth to the genius which in turn produced the machinery of production and distribution by means of which they are now enslaved to the monster of monsters—unemployment.

How many inventions are the products of the minds of the rich, exploiting aristocrat? The writer knows of none.

The common people, their sons and daughters were the artisans who laid the stones of the progress of civilization. They have been the builders only to be exploited for their efforts. The creators of wealth only to lose it to the exploiter. Exploitation and graft are the products of the dreams of the idle rich who seek to grow fat on the blood of their brothers.

The middle class common people of today are dreaming dreams of an age when graft and exploitation shall no longer enslave the race. Dreaming dreams of a new day when the wheat shall be separated from the chaff; of a future where purity, justice and truth shall rule, and where the aristocracy of idleness shall have perished from the earth and man shall at last be free.

504741

"Thrones have crumbled and kings are dust" at the hands of the common class.

Human thought once born never dies. The originator of the thought may be placed behind prison walls, he may be buried beneath the sod, but the thought that is born of him, if pure, wholesome and righteous, for the happiness of man, will live on and grow like the seed in the soil, only to reproduce itself time and again until its influence reaches deep into the hearts and minds of men.

Millions of the common class are dreaming dreams of a new day and a new deal.

Capitalists dreaming dreams of more exploitation resist even the efforts of the President of the United States to plant the seeds of justice in the soil of government itself. They may resist the President and destroy his efforts. They cannot resist the common class for long. The kinddom of wealth is crumbling.

The common masses are dreaming dreams of a leader to lead them out of a land of confusion and to rule by reason and justice. They will find one. The hour has struck.

CHAPTER VIII.

The Natural Laws

Certain fundamental laws of nature have had a decided influence upon the dreams, the hopes, the aspirations and the conduct of man.

The law of self-preservation; natural selection; following paths of least resistance; just compensation, and the law of the survival of the fittest.

Failure to understand and apply these laws properly have occasioned man nothing but heartaches, pain, misery and suffering. Time was, when man lived under conditions wherein the instinct of self-preservation required him to kill in order to live.

Times have changed. Centuries have passed, and theoretically at any rate, man has progressed.

Society has been complex. Productive methods efficient. Industrial activity interwoven into every function of human life.

Now, in order to preserve ourselves we must preserve others, in order to be happy we must make others happy. We can help ourselves only by helping others. Today proper application of the law of self-preservation is to be found in the golden rule. Only the exploiter now practices the law of self-preservation as it was practiced centuries ago. It makes no difference whether the killing was done by means of a crude club or whether modern methods of cornering wealth by a few greedy, gluttonous individuals accomplishes the killing by starvation. Perhaps the savage method was the less cruel.

Nor does it matter whether the physical body is killed or whether the modern method of exploitation, graft and greed merely kills life that lives in the soul, burned out by the fires of hatred. Better had the body be killed first in order that the soul may be liberated to return to its Creator.

Greed for gold is a terrible monster in the lives of men and turns them into savage beasts that cannot even hear the cries of hunger on the part of the little children.

The law of natural selection, wherein only the physical aspects of life have been the ruling force of the past, has created havoc in the development of civilization and of the race.

Spiritual and mental attributes of life are more important to the race and its future than is the physical side of life, for when vision ceases, life perishes.

Man carefully selects the progenitors of a dairy herd. He develops a race of live stock on the farm with the utmost care. The result of his efforts are finer breeds of cattle, hogs, horses and sheep. Better strains and better races.

Man, with utter carelessness, allows the mentally weak, the physically diseased and criminally inclined to reproduce, only to bring into the world more misery, poverty, want and suffering. Strange but sadly true.

The tendency to follow the path of least resistance has throughout the ages been the millstone on the neck of man. That which causes him to take what he can get with the least effort and to just drift along. He may complain about it bitterly, but complaints do not fill empty stomachs. The present lot of man may be a bitter one but he made it for himself. He is its father and it his child. His lot will ever be thus until he makes sufficient progress to resist wrongs and fight for the right. Right is within his grasp if he will get on his two feet and reach out for it. The law giver Moses gave him the code. It is his to follow. It is his to require others to follow.

The survival of the fittest confers upon no class or group the right to exploit another class or group simply because of wealth they may attain a sufficient amount of power in government to do so.

Natural laws are for the animal kingdom. God gave man a mind and intended that he use it. He gave him a conscience by which he can measure right and wrong. Intellect must be made a living force in charting the course of the race. Mind must govern matter; intelligence must govern faith and right must be made might. Right must be the controlling power of government, of law, of life. When this comes to pass, stock market crashes will not occur only to produce starvation; only to transfer wealth from the middle class to the aristocrat. Greed and gold will no longer stalk through legislative halls as an octopus, strangling the lives of millions.

When right everywhere is made the master of might, the dream of Him whom they crucified will have come true. Poverty and want will be no more and man can lift his face toward the shining sun and truly say, "I am a man in the likeness of my Creator."

CHAPTER IX.

Economics

In times of stress and strain when there is much discourse on the subject of economics, we wonder just what the field of economics covers. As we analyze it, it comprehends the science of investigation, management of the affairs of government as regards its source of income, its expenditures, the development of its natural resources and the investigation and management of conditions affecting production, distribution and consumption of wealth or the material means of satisfying human desires and human wants, food, clothing, shelter, education and luxuries of life. It also comprehends the organization of the industrial, financial and commercial enterprises into such shape and form that they may produce the greatest good to the greatest number.

We have these economic institutions now, organized it is claimed by the greatest brain power the world has ever developed, and yet there exists chaos and confusion, turmoil and bewilderment that baffles the most expert economists of the day. The confusion and distress grows out of the fact that commodities, food, clothing and shelter, have not been produced for use, but have been made for profit. In order to create a successful economic system, it is necessary that human needs, wants and desires are created by industries for use without the attendant abuses created by selfishness. In other words, our industrial system and economic life must be made to conform with human needs rather than to the desires of the profiteers.

When agriculture plants or sows its grain in a natural environment, where topographical soils and climatic conditions are correct, taking into account the distribution and consumption of the produce; when the lands unfit for growing grain are used for grazing lands; when our mills and factories are built in localities where most needed, without being based upon profit and exploitation; when distribution of commodities and service is made without the evil effects of cut-throat competition; transportation whether by rail or road is organized in the light of need, owned and operated by those whom they are intended to serve; when these things come to pass, the economist can stand on the mountain of intelligence and look down into the valleys of contentment, peace and plenty. These things cannot come to pass so long as basic enterprises of the nation, the natural resources of the soil, such as coal, water power, utility service and transportation, are owned by selfish interests, operated for selfish profit, adding cost to the consumer and breeding inefficiency in operation. Basic enterprises must be owned and operated by the people for a common good. Financial institutions and banks owned, controlled and operated by the government for the good of its people and not for Wall Street. Political offices must be filled with the best minds, possessing knowledge of agriculture, industry, finance, and above all things, a knowledge of life. The resources of a great nation should be pleasing to the people inhabiting it. It can be made pleasing to those but only by honesty, efficiency, charity and integrity in their regulation, control and ownership by this institution which we designate as government.

CHAPTER X

Banks and Banking

It is not the purpose of this chapter to treat the banking or currency question beyond mere suggestion. To do so would require a complete book.

First, money is not value. It represents, theoretically, value. It is merely a medium of exchange whereby a day's labor may be exchanged for a bushel of potatoes, a sack of flour, a side of pork and the like without the necessity of the laborer finding some farmer with those particular items to exchange, one who needs a day's labor.

It is the circulation media whereby in this complex society the exchanges may be facilitated.

Under the Constitution Congress has the power to coin money and to regulate the value thereof.

There is much loose talk about fiat money, yet the value of every dollar we now have or ever have had has been and is fixed by legislative fiat or command by the enactment of law. This talk is the bogy man which is used to frighten the unwary and unsuspecting.

Secondly, money being the medium of exchange only, for a great nation, should be owned by the government. Most people now believe it is. It is in fact owned by the banks, hence the banks have control of the life-blood of commercial intercourse of an entire nation.

Bank failures have proven conclusively that endless disaster to commerce and human life itself follows in the train of maladministration of the banking enterprise. When the life-blood ceases to flow the commercial body of the nation sickens. It has been terribly sick and came to the portals of death's door before anyone made any effort to effect a cure.

Banks, by depositing United States Bonds with the Treasury Department, may have issued to them currency at one-half per cent interest plus the nominal cost of printing, which they loan out to the public at seven or eight per cent interest. While the bonds are on deposit the banks continue to collect the interest payments on them.

Their practice is lawful, though morally wicked. They have a legal right to the interest rates but morally they practice usury in the grossest form.

We are approaching an age where compensation must be based upon service. What service have the banks rendered by loaning money given them by the Government at a high rate of interest beyond the extension of an unsound credit and bringing to the home owner and the nation bankruptcy? Not an achievement to be proud of. "Consult your Banker" used to be the slogan. No longer is it true. Too many of us cannot afford to travel to Leavenworth or Atlanta, Georgia, in order to consult our bankers.

We are told that there is about nine billions of dollars in money, issued in the United States, and about one-third of it hidden by the hoarder.

Interest payments alone exacted by the bankers each year exceed the total of all the money issued in the United States.

They are collecting interest on money loaned. There is not that much money to loan. They loan the credit of their depositors, and on their depositors' credit collect interest.

Debts created and in existence, public and private, are twenty times the amount of money there is in existence to pay them. They will not, they cannot be paid under the present banking and monetary system.

Banks will eventually be owned by the government. Money will be owned by the government. The medium of exchange will be used for the benefit of the nation. When this comes to pass the stock market and Wall Street crapshooters will no longer be able over night, by manipulation, to upset the economic equilibrium of an entire nation.

Let it come soon. How soon depends on how much intelligence we use at the ballot box.

CHAPTER XI.

Insurance

Human life, with its tragedies, requires availability of some form of security or protection for the family.

Insurance has been the answer. It originated centuries ago in the coffee houses of England where men laid wagers on the safe delivery of a ship cargo across the stormy seas.

It has extended into every avenue of life, even to wagering the premiums paid against a future span of years of the life of the assured.

Life insurance companies have wagered well and have developed a financial power and strength which enabled them, better than any other institution, to weather the storms of depression. They now vie with the International Banker for first position in financial power. A power gained by methods which have been accompanied by scandals and indefensible procedure. The element of exploitation has not been absent in their growth.

"What nobler deed could man perform, than to take care of that priceless gem, the mother. Care for her, when he, who had pledged his care, has gone to rest, or care for that feeble mind, who's strong hands once helped shape the path that we must walk, or care for that little mind, who, some future day, will strew, upon this same path, thorns or roses, according to his molded whims.''

Insurance companies have saved thousands on the one hand during the depression, yet on the other as a result of real estate gambling, have taken farms and homes, and are fast becoming the land owning autocracy of America. Are we now taking the first step toward agricultural peonage under the control of land owning insurance companies? Only time can answer the question.

Insurance is one of the most satisfying of all investments as one passes through death's portals, yet these vast fortunes have been built at the expense of the public. The public always pays.

The system has its weakness in the field of industrial insurance which is the most pernicious of any single enterprise in America. After forty you are a bad insurance risk. Industry finds reason for discharge from service. After forty you cannot find employment because you increase the rate of premium required. In the prime of productive life, yet unwanted. A sad commentary on the insurance business. Shall we shoot men over forty?

There is a better and more humane way. Insurance, and particularly in industry, is a quasi public utility. Service and not profit should be the foundation upon which to build. Men over forty must be maintained by someone. When everyone else fails, the taxpayer, through government, must care for the unemployed. Far better would it be for the government to own and operate the industrial insurance field. It is the only solution. Let it be done before unemployment destroys the nation.

CHAPTER XII.

The Industrial Field

Too often problems of life are treated as moral problems. Every problem in American life, of any consequence, is, at bottom, an economic problem. Out of economic problems of the past, we have developed a civilization. In the maze of industrial economic problems today, we seek to save a civilization. It is in the field of industry that the things we need, desire, and want, are made.

The industrial field has grown from a craftsmanship of human hands and human skill, to a modern giant of complicated machinery, designed for mass production. Today the major part of our civilization must procure their livelihood in the field of industry, hence the welfare, happiness, progress and advancement of humankind of the state and nation, and all society itself, is dependent upon the administration and operation of industry.

We have erroneously assumed that the land and natural resources are wealth. Land is worth nothing, nor the ore or coal in the ground, until the brain and hands of man shape them into

51

useful articles needed in life. Industry started as a number of individual enterprises, and like many other things, has fallen within the tentacles of the bankers, for the purpose of creating their own wealth and adding thereto, rather than rendering service to society. Profit, profit, and more profit, all built upon the idea of exploiting humankind.

Helpless have the people been in the hands of the industrialists, with little to say as to what they should receive for the labor in producing the goods, and less to say as to what they should pay for the goods which their efforts produced. Little to say as to where, when, or for whom they should work. Life has become hard and millions have been unwillingly made industrial slaves by the fear of starvation and want. This system has grown throughout the years, by the cunning of the industrialists in legislative halls, where special favor was sought and obtained, where special privilege could be bought at a price, which price was always in turn paid by those who made and those who consumed the products of industry. Industrial heads far removed from their plants themselves, gradually came to look upon the men employed as mere machines, to be discarded at will, if a few more cents' profit could be made in the process. Not only has the industrialists spread his tentacles over America, but he has extended them out into the remainder of the world, where $150,000,000,-000 of foreign capital are invested in the production of goods in America. This means, that we are feeding, clothing and housing in magnificent splendor the princes and nobles of Europe while we here at home are starving, wearing rags and living in hovels.

In normal times there are employed in the United States approximately 40,000,000 of people, paid in wages and salaries, from $15,000,-000,000 to $20,000,000,000 per year. These people produce $100,000,000,000 worth of commodities, a $75,000,000,000 or $80,000,000,000 differential between the labor cost and the cost to the consumer. The first step toward social control and regulation in industry has been taken by enactment of the National Industrial Recovery Law. No longer can industry be permitted in America to run wild and carry out to savage purposes, for the sake of profit. The preservation of society is at stake. If the industrialists have not sense enough to preserve it of their own initiative, the people will preserve it for themselves. The first step has now been taken. The industrialist might well look to the future, take an inventory of his own conscience before he drives the nation into a system of public ownership of industry itself. Millions of dollars of bonus to executive heads in industry cannot be justified, while people starve for want of food.

The operating cost of Government has been approximately $20,000,000,000 a year. The income tax reports of the Government discloses that many men pay taxes on incomes of over $1,000,000 per year and thousands pay taxes on incomes of more than $100,000 per year, on incomes produced from profits made by service rendered by those who produce and create the wealth. When the tax is paid, an overhead charge item goes on the books to be paid by the combined effort of those who produce next year's goods and those who consume them, indirectly.

The continuance of greed and selfishness in the management of industry can and will lead to only one result. Public punishment can be borne so long, but when the system becomes too burdensome they will refuse to be driven further. This refusal may manifest itself in public ownership, which the industrialists seek to avoid; it is in their hands to avoid, if they but will. The path is open, the way is clear. A fair distribution of the result of effort on the part of the producer, and a fair assumption of the tax obligations for the support of the Government as a corollary for the protection which the Government provides for industry.

CHAPTER XIII.

The Commercial Field

Commerce is almost as old as the race. That, like industry, began as an individual enterprise. It comprises the distribution and exchange of commodities and service among men. With the development of a complex industrial system came the development of a highly organized commericial nation. In this commercial nation there has been established between the producer and the consumer, an endless chain of salesmen, jobbers, wholesalers, and the like, rendering no service beyond that of keeping books. This has given rise to propaganda which we designate as advertising, most of which is false, for the purpose of creating desires which the common man cannot possibly satisfy and enriching those who already control the nation's resources.

The most iniquitous of all development in the commercial field is unquestionably the chain store system, owned by capital far removed from the community wherein each day's receipts are immediately forwarded to New York City, removing the money from the community where the particular store is situated. By a gradual process of the transfer of profits, there has come the gradual transfer of more wealth to Wall Street, while out in the cities, towns and hamlets of America there is not a sufficient amount of money in circulation to satisfy even the barest and simplest needs of life. This field too must come in for regulation and control by Government, for the preservation of society. The Government operates a Post Office in every city and town in America. It sells its service for a price, but does not set up on the opposite side of the street another Post Office, to enter into competition, and then try to create by advertising, a service which is not wanted nor needed by the public. The chain store has destroyed initiative, wiped out individual opportunity, and rendered impossible the establishment of a boy in business, wherein he can become an asset to the community, be self-sustaining, render a service at a fair compensation. Driven to extremes, we may find more than Governmental control, in that there may be developed community owned stores, operated not for profit, but for service. This may not be so remote as at first glance it appears to be. The first step has already been taken by the farmer, in the establishment of their community stores in all corners of the United States.

The important thing is not who performs the operation or the service, but rather that in the performance thereof, happiness and contentment may be brought into the lives of our people.

CHAPTER XIV.

The Political Field

The germ of the Government of the United States was expressed in the preamble to the Declaration of Independence in the definition of the inalienable rights, as being the right to life, liberty and the pursuit of happiness.

In order to give expression to those rights, in concrete form, the constitution created a plan of Government and established a Republic, emanating directly from the people, to be controlled by them, through their duly elected representatives.

Political parties are extra constitutional institutions naturally developed as the result of the plan and party government, but although extra constitutional institutions they have become as much a part of the plan as the plan itself. Therefore the Political field encompasses an organized method of Government of the people by the people themselves. In its inception, there was created the most splendid Government ever produced by the mind of man.

Through no fault of the plan or purpose has there been any failure. Corruption has arisen in the extra constitutional party form of Government, under the leadership of selfish and unscrupulous politicians, giving rise to exploitation and graft, two elements never contemplated by the plan itself.

The purpose of the plan was to execute the will of the people, but the purpose has been distorted until party platforms and campaign pledges have become merely vote capturers, to be forgotten immediately after the passing of the oath of office from the lips of the office holder.

Obligations created during campaigns, by financial assistance and pledge of votes, have given rise to unjust laws, conferring of special privileges to special classes, increasing tax burdens and destroying confidence in Government.

In 1819 the greatest jurist ever produced by America, Chief Justice John Marshall, said that all apparent differences in Governmental problems could be cured by the magic of the word "Confidence". Confidence has been the premise upon which our Government has rested. Confidence has been lost and almost entirely destroyed. During this four (4) years of depression, confidence in Government, in finance, in industry, in society, and even in fellowmen, has been submerged in the distress of despair. Bewilderment and confusion prevail; industry is at a standstill, and no one able to set in motion the machinery of production and distribution. Billions have been distributed to relieve distress and yet at this writing, 10,000,000 men are unemployed; if we allow three (3) to a family, 30,000,000 in distress, or four (4) to a family, one-third (1/3) of our population on the brink of despair. Purchasing power is gone and no one seems to be able to place any money into the hands of the common people, in order that they may satisfy their wants. Our political system has developed demagogues and demagoguery has become the rule in Political life.

On the other hand the voters are subject to the criticism that party ties are stronger to them than honesty and integrity of man, subject to the criticism that they rely more on promises made by office seekers than they do upon measuring the man by past conduct and integrity before seeking office, subject to the criticism that they do not vote at all, subject to the criticism that they have made no sincere effort to learn even the fundamental principles of Politics, or to acquire a fair understanding of Government, and its operation, and the tax burdens incident thereto.

The right to be a sovereign citizen was granted by the constitution, and to be a sovereign citizen, the voter must become an intelligent citizen. When intelligence prevails, demagoguery, of necessity, dies. Where an accounting is required, bad faith on the part of office holders will cease to exist. When there shall arise in our people a conscience which will make politicians and office holders fear guilt and censure more than punishment, many of our political difficulties will solve themselves. Equality of opportunity and equality before the law, special privilege to none, must be made a living force, if party government shall survive and the present form prevail.

CHAPTER XV.

Agriculture

Those who provide the nation with bread and food have suffered most during these years of depression. For agriculture, the depression began ten (10) years ago, notwithstanding the fact the very lives of our people depended upon it for physical existence.

Considering the investment owned by the farmer, the hours of toil in his enterprise, he has been the most poorly paid class of all classes in the nation, yet it comprises one-third (1/3) of our population. He has been deprived of a purchasing power for ten (10) years, substantially one-third (1/3) of our population has been out of the market, therefore the laborer in the factory could produce nothing for him. He had nothing with which to buy the products of labor.

On account of the individualistic spirit of the farmer, and the wide separation of the farmers as a group, it has been impossible for them to build an organization through which to speak and act. He has been promised more and lied to more than any class in America. Political parties have promised relief year after year, yet organized minorities grasping for more wealth have thwarted the promises. Effort has been made to correlate the movements of labor and agriculture. Difficult is this to do, because the interests conflict. If the farmer gets a high price for his produce, labor must use more of its earnings with which to buy food hence the lower the price of farm produce, the further will the laborer's dollar reach.

This is perhaps the first time in the history of the nation when land and improvements had a value of less than the improvements themselves. Effort is now being made, through the Department of Agriculture, to assist the farmer in organization and in curtailment of production, in order that surplus may be removed and fair prices received. Much can be done in this direction by the elimination of middle men whose service consists of bookkeeping, resulting in low prices to the farmer and high prices to the consumer.

Ten cents worth of grain from the farmer, when produced into a breakfast food, is brought to the consumer at the price of $1.00.

The farmer may get 2½ cents a quart for his milk, but when delivered at the door of the consumer, it costs 10 cents.

Five bushels of wheat produce a barrel of flour with the miller retaining the bran and middlings for sale. The barrel of flour will produce 320 one and one-half pound loaves of bread. At 50 cents per bushel, the farmer gets $2.50 for the wheat and the consumer pays $32.00 for the bread, which the wheat produces.

Farm machinery manufacturers have exploited the farmer by excessive cost of farm machinery. While dollars are the medium of exchange for the farmer, for convenience, the only true medium of exchange is his wheat, corn, oats, and the produce of his farm. It is not how many dollars he must pay for a binder, but how many bushels of wheat must he exchange to obtain the machine.

The agriculture industry must not be destroyed. The farmer hewed down the forest, built the roads, transformed the prairies, and was the base upon which the nation was built. It was the farmer who created America, and who has fought every war in her defense. It is not impossible at all that the safety of the farmer may lay in disregarding economic laws and fixing the price of farm produce, by legislative enactment, just as congress has fixed the price of coal. Disorganized agriculture can do nothing. Organized, it can control the policies of the nation.

CHAPTER XVI.

Christianity

When man was created, he was given intellect. It is that characteristic which distinguishes him from the animal kingdom. The power to think and the power to reason. It is that instinct and that power which has created of him a worshiper. It is that attribute which has caused him to give recognition to the fact that the greatest code of ethics ever produced came down to him through the ages, from the Great Law Giver, away back in the dim, distant past, from the rugged brow of Mount Sinai. A code of ethics giving recognition to a common fatherhood, a universal brotherhood, the golden rule, love of man. In this great code of ethics, commonly known as the Ten Commandments, love and human helpfulness is the golden thread. Exploitation is repugnant to the entire code.

Many now claim there are no christians, that there is no christian nation, that the only place christianity has in the lives of the people is in theory, but not in practice. In that code of ethics can be found the central idea amply sufficient and adequate for the regulation of human conduct in any government. Moses found need for only ten (10) laws. We now have some two million, because of the waywardness of mankind and the refusal to conform to the Ten Commandments.

Men pray to their God on Sunday, prey upon their neighbors during six (6) days of the week and bray at all times about their christianity. Never was a war fought which did not violate the Ten Commandments, and particularly that Commandment, "Thou shalt not kill". In principle, there is little difference whether, with a gun placed in the pit of the stomach of a fellow-man, a dollar is extracted from his pocket, or whether it is extracted in the darkness of the night secretly, or whether it is extracted by exploitation, simply because the law permits it to be done.

Every race, whether civilized or uncivilized, had a religion of some character. Whether it was based upon Ten Commandments or based upon fear and superstition, man has always recognized some power beyond and above him. The instinct to worship has always been present within his soul. What lies beyond the grave has always held a certain amount of terror for him, and out of this terror there has been painted for him pictures in after life, of music, harps, and stairs of gold, even by those who direct the religious thought of mankind. What a powerful and tremendous influence gold, cold and yellow, has had upon man throughout the ages.

The purification of the soul or the humanization of man, for man's sake, is the base of true religion. Truth, honor and justice practiced in life must of certainty bring the reward hereafter, if there is any reward to be found. Starving bodies produce hatred, starving bodies stint the soul. Fear and discontent destroy the peace, love and loyalty that is essential to the building of a Christian Civilization.

CHAPTER XVII.

Recapitulation 1

Man, who by thought and action created science, art, literature, machinery, and filled warehouses to overflowing with food and clothing, has now reached a point where privation borders on starvation in the midst of plenty and to spare, because in his individualistic attitude of mind and selfishness he has been unwilling to correlate individual welfare with group welfare.

He has permitted bankers, industrialists, commercialists, and politicians to lead him and exploit him until he now stands at the crossroads of progress and decay. Which road will he take? The common ownership of the natural resources, the land, finance, machinery, industry and governmental regulation of production and distribution for the welfare of all the people, is his only hope. The home must be reestablished, the character builded from the first day of life. In the distribution with mass production, hours of labor must be reduced and incomes retained where all men shall not only enjoy the necessities of life, but will be able to enjoy the luxuries thereof. Society must be organized so that men rendering no service cannot live at the expense of others. Industrial insurance must be provided by Government, in order that man may be protected in case of accident, illness, and in old age and death. Educational opportunities and facilities must be extended in the development of an intelligent race, capable of ruling by reason rather than by sword, force and exploitation. By united action, justice, truth and love must be reestablished. Our nation, the melting pot of the world, must be blended into a nation of liberty, equality and justice. In a nation as rich as ours, with the resources we possess, there should be found human enterprise sufficient to organize the problems of distribution and production so that we can truly sing in unison: "America the Beautiful", "Undimmed by human tears".

CHAPTER XVIII.

Recapitulation 2

Man, who has by thought and action, with his artistic intellect, produced science, art and literature; who has with his genius and skill originated machinery of production and distribution to take the place of manual labor; who has, by mass production, filled the warehouses to overflowing with food and clothing, with necessities and luxuries, has actually come to a stage of privation that borders on starvation, just because he never was interested in his private or individual welfare from a collective point of consideration. He has permitted bankers, industrialists, commercialists and politicians to lead him, exploit him, to determine his every existence, until today he is facing ruination and decay. His only hope is the common ownership of the productive machinery of production and distribution, the banks and the medium of exchange, the natural resources and the land. His only salvation is, to do himself what he had entrusted to others, pull himself out of the mire that his enemies have prepared for him.

Woman, too, must help to pull man out of the depth of his despair, so that he can help her to attain the position in life that is rightfully hers. Help her out of sweat shops, out of industrial and commercial institutions so that she can promote that which is by nature her heritage, making the home, giving civilization children, free from the effects of heavy drudgery, which produces hollow eyes, stooped shoulders, and stupid minds. Recruiting thousands into the brothels of our red light districts. Take out of twenty million homes the cook stove and build massive dining halls operated for the communities and not for private profit, so that food will be dispensed, wholesome and balanced, for the health and strength of all.

Take away the wash board and tub and the ironing board. Have modern laundries scientifically operated for the people. The experience of the past, prehistorical and historical, will be the guiding influence that will lead us to civilization's loftiest grandeur.

In the economic field we will develop conditions fitting to our surroundings, increase mass production, reduce the hours of labor and have an income corresponding to our production. Thus, we will be able to satisfy our desires and be governed entirely by the law of supply and demand, where we have now the law of manipulation.

We will forever abolish interest and profit, so no man can live at the expense of another. Giving every one an opportunity to own a home and when that home is established no power on earth can take it, not even the state or the federal government.

When a child is born, it automatically becomes insured by the state, systematically covering every form of liability, so it matters not what happens, you are protected by the state, be it an accident, sickness, old age, or death. The premium on this insurance would be a small amount on account of the fact that most of the overhead expense would be eliminated, such as numerous companies, agents, officials, offices, etc.

As an example, let us just analyze one situation in the insurance department. Today, when one becomes too old or feeble to work, he is a subject of charity. He must go to his children or go to the poor house for services without recompense. Let us take it for granted that he has dutiful children. They provide him with the care he needs. Does he not realize that he is a burden and actually takes bread out of his children's mouths? On the other hand, let him receive a compensation for life. He at once becomes desirable. Every child wants him and will take the best of care of him, for the longer he lives the better, and he himself feels the importance; he feels that he is not a burden but an important factor in the welfare of all concerned.

His grandchildren also see the care their parents give to the grandparents, and thus kindness and care for the aged and weak, filial love would in a few generations become a second nature, creating an environment that would create a good heredity.

We would have all children at school and college until they become of age, so they would become fit to take up the burden of life. Then too, did not one of our greatest poets say: "Many a beautiful flower blossoms forth, behind some rubbish pile, and then withers and dies, unknown and unnoticed."

Keep them out of the economic fields until they are trained for the task. Also take them out at an early age, by an old age compensation, so that a useful life would enjoy the fruits of its labors in the declining years of its career and only the physically fit will serve society, which would make work a delight and life a pleasure.

Our farms would be operated by a common ownership and the farmer, who is and must be a skilled workman, would be paid the same as others. He would work short hours and receive a just compensation, thereby making the farmer a peer in our economic system, prosperous, happy and contented.

In all of these enterprises we would be following the principles of the Nazarene, the Prince of Peace.

The brotherhood of man will never begin, until we, by united action, start it with justice, truth and love as our guide.

We, here in America, are indeed expected to do much, for here we find a new civilization, a race built of the best blood of all lands. A melting pot of the most aggressive, fearless, individuals of all the nations of the earth. Here the hot blooded Spaniard and the cold-blooded Nordic, the sturdy German and the crafty Frenchman, the Englishman, the Irishman, the Scotchman, and the Welchman, in fact, all the civilized races of the whole world are commingled by a common consent, producing the finest blood on earth.

Through all of these bloods runs the blood of Israel, God's chosen people.

The true Israelites, the descendants of Abraham, became christianized and their blood flows in our veins. Therefore, we are expected to lead the world to the goal that God promised Israel, down through the ages. "A land of Promise, God's kingdom, where we pray Thy Kingdom come, Thy will be done, on earth as it is in heaven." Where we will say to the tempter: "Begone, Satan, this is my Father's kingdom."

CHAPTER XIX.

An Appeal

At present American civilization is standing on the ruins and ashes of an economic system which has impoverished her people. A system built on greed. A system wild, free, uncontrolled and indomitably selfish. Never has there been any national planning of that which most vitally affects the lives of a people, the development of its economic structure.

Under our system of government regulation control of industry and finance must come from the government itself. The first step has been taken. Coming from the government it comes from its officers and statesmen—if there be any left.

To those who rule we say—look out upon those who produce, yet live in poverty, now dreaming dreams. Paper titles no longer impress them. They are living in despair. They look to you.

The nation can and will be lifted out of the mire of selfishness. America will be saved. She will be saved by the class which made her a great nation. America will be free. She will be happy. Greed will be submerged in fine ideals. Those who stand at the wheel of the ship of State can lead the movement if they will. If not, a leader will be found. Sadness, grief and starvation will not be tolerated.

Just a short time ago, I stood at the bier of a baby. A baby dead of malnutrition (slow starvation) caused by lack of food.

While standing there I saw that mother, silently weeping for her lost child, broken hearted, hopeless. I saw the father, young, handsome and strong, standing, pale, tearless, desperate. Something seemed to be tearing at his heart as he looked upon that tiny, emaciated body, his dead baby. Dead—through no fault of his own; dead from lack of food,—food that he could not provide, when warehouses and stores are filled with all the food needed and the government paying the producers of food for not sowing seed for food and clothing.

As I looked upon this sad scene of suffering, grief and sorrow, my imagination looked back just a few years, when this same mother as a happy, carefree maiden, filled with hope and confidence, gave her heart and hand to this young man, little dreaming that she would see her baby, her own flesh and blood, the victim of an unjust system, crushed, murdered by the folly and madness of blind greed.

In my meditations, I saw back in history Socrates pinning flowers on the breasts of the youths of Greece and telling them of a glorious world to be. He was compelled to drink poison hemlock and die for his effort.

I saw Sparticus, the Roman slave, lead seventy thousand of his fellow slaves to an illustrious death, forever banishing white slavery.

I saw the Christ suffer a cruel, agonizing death for teaching love, a world brotherhood, peace and good will.

I saw Jean Val Jean, with a heart of gold, serve nineteen years in prison for stealing a loaf of bread for his sister's starving children, then come out of prison with a heart of stone, robbing, plundering and killing, throwing a whole nation into shambles.

I saw the queen of that same nation, when they told her that the peasants had no bread, tell them to eat cake, then saw her head fall in the basket of the guillotine.

I saw Washington and his ragged army, at Valley Forge, freezing, starving, bleeding and dying, so that a mighty nation could prosper and be free.

I saw Lincoln, the great emancipator of the black slave, stand as a hero in the eyes of millions.

I saw Armistice Day, the conclusion of the wholesale destruction of life and property in a

World War. I saw men and women, old and young, rich and poor, married and single, all unite in making merry, for a national distress and anxiety that was dispelled.

Now we look upon the picture reversed. Careworn expressions on the faces of people as they walk restlessly to and fro upon the streets. What, let us ask, would be the result should they turn to violence? Do we know they will not? Emphatically we do not know.

Hark ye! Statesmen! Rulers! Masters! Listen to the rumblings of unrest! Look upon the drab picture of suffering. Act, not tomorrow, next week, next month, next year. Act now. Tomorrow may be too late.

The world waits to be remade. Civilization truly is on trial. You are its defenders, its counsellors. The common mass of men and women, the jury. They will return the verdict in no uncertain terms.

CHAPTER XX.

Organization

We have conquered land, sea and air. We have enslaved the forces of nature to be the tireless, ceaseless toilers for the whole human race. We have brought human labor from an aimless drudge to a well regulated science, functioning in every activity almost to perfection.

Physical man has become a peer, a king in the industrial and commercial world. From primitive life he has brought us to a beautiful world, a world filled with desires, necessities and luxuries, but unevenly distributed.

Intellectual man must learn to distribute equally the greatest of all desires, opportunity.

In order to do this, he must cooperate, organize in every field of activity that has the power to govern, produce and distribute, and fight with the most powerful weapon the world ever knew, the power invested in us by the builders of this mighty nation, the ballot.

With the ballot we can bring the benighted political field up to an economic standard, so it will conform and function with our modern environments.

The ballot, if used, will repeal all unjust laws and replace them with just laws. It will create conditions that will make life worth living. It can place the banks in the hands of the government, start the mints in making metallic money, start the bureau of printing and engraving, making greenbacks in amounts adequate for human trade and commerce.

Start the mills and the mines, the farms and the factories, and pay the workers who work with brains or brawn with this money, for services rendered. Pay each person working enough to buy commodities at prevailing prices so that every honorable human want could be satisfied. Let no one work more than four hours per day, five days per week. With modern methods properly directed it will suffice.

Let everything bought have the government stamp upon it for purity, quality, quantity, price, the cost of production and distribution.

All this and more you can get for your vote. To do this there must be numerical strength, unity and righteousness of purpose and plan.

Not by faith alone, but by faith and action will Christianity and economic justice be reborn.

It matters not whether you are a Catholic, Protestant, Jew, Infidel, Agnostic, or Atheist, you believe in a principle that is right, just and truthful.

It matters not whether you are a Republican, Democrat, or Socialist. We all are Republicans, for we believe in a republican form of government. We all are Democrats, for we believe in the democratic management of statehood and we all must become Socialists, for the time has come when the social regulation of all productive industries must be a reality so that the common people can no longer be exploited by a few, for a few.

Consecrate your life to the principle of a Christian Democracy, so you can hold up your hands at all times and say: "My hands are clean, I am not guilty of perpetuating the present system."

You have nothing to lose, and a world to gain. A world of dreams and possibilities. A world where childhood is personified by maturity. A world where the declining years of age is likened to a glorious sunset. A world where youth, age and beauty will romp and play as children play. Where the strong will protect the weak, and where all mankind will guard happiness until the end of time.

CHAPTER XXI.

Conclusion

A world in the making. In the beginning there was nothing but gaseous matter. Then the earth was formed. It matters not whether it was formed in one day or whether it was done by evolution or revolution—it was done.

The mountains and the valleys, the cliffs and the rocks show us that it was not an easy, smooth task, but an arduous one, with calamities and catastrophies galore.

When the proper time came, vegetation appeared, feeding and thriving on the matter that had solidified. When vegetation was firmly started, animal life appeared. It fed on vegetation and developed, like vegetation, by the natural laws, cross-breeding and hybridization. Thus the mineral kingdom, the vegetable kingdom and the animal kingdom were established.

Man also came—it matters not whether he came instantaneously or whether he was produced by evolution and revolution, by cross breeding or hybridization. What does matter is, how he has lived, how he lives now, and how he will live. What method he has used, what method he uses now, and what method he should and will use in the future to procure food, clothing and shelter.

The mineral, the vegetable and the animal kingdoms have developed from an infancy to their present stage. Man, too, has developed from an infancy to his present stage. Man's method of procuring food and necessities also has developed from an infancy to the present stage.

A child develops from an infant to maturity, going through the various stages by degrees, every stage full of fear, anxiety and danger, ever guided by hope and expectancy.

So, too, did the human race go from stage to stage, by evolution and revolution, through the various stages of its career, every stage full of fear, anxiety and danger, ever guided by hope and expectancy.

So, too, does the method of procuring food and necessities develop from one stage to another, from the crude to an artful skill, from the simple to the complex.

So, too, does society develop from the crude, savage to the present, always going to a higher stage, from one civilization to another, guided by the method of procuring food and necessities.

Our civilization seems to have stopped; confusion is everywhere. The best minds are perplexed. Governments are trembling and all mankind is helpless.

The whole atmosphere seems to be charged with a longing. A longing for a new deal—a new civilization.

Stupidity and greed have made us forget the teachings and warnings of the prophets, the sages and the Christ, and now we stand on the brink of the abyss of darkness. While over it all, hanging like a pall, hovers the hideous monster, WAR. If we seek and find the truth, we will safely and sanely pass the crisis. If we neglect to do our part, then blood and tears will be our reward.

How and when we do not know. Great reforms are born of sorrow and suffering. Civilization pauses in her path of progress. She is on trial. She stands mute. Millions wait silently, haunted by the spectre of want caused by greed.

With God in His heaven and hope in the hearts of men, love, honor, truth and justice will prevail.

The answer rests with the people. Let it be answered "firmly in the right as God gives us LIGHT to see the right", and let it be answered now.

THE END